Welcome To The Camper
Guest Book

Host:

Start Date:

Copyright 2018
Amberly Books

Name:
Date:
Hometown:

Message:

Name:
Date:
Hometown:

Message:

Name:
Date:
Hometown:

Message:

Name:
Date:
Hometown:

Message:

Name:
Date:
Hometown:

Message:

Name:
Date:
Hometown:

Message:

Name:
Date:
Hometown:

Message:

Name:
Date:
Hometown:

Message:

Name:
Date:
Hometown:

Message:

Name:
Date:
Hometown:

Message:

Name:
Date:
Hometown:

Message:

Name:
Date:
Hometown:

Message:

Name:
Date:
Hometown:

Message:

Name:
Date:
Hometown:

Message:

Name:
Date:
Hometown:

Message:

Name:
Date:
Hometown:

Message:

Name:
Date:
Hometown:

Message:

Name:
Date:
Hometown:

Message:

Name:
Date:
Hometown:

Message:

Name:
Date:
Hometown:

Message:

Name:
Date:
Hometown:

Message:

Name:
Date:
Hometown:

Message:

Name:
Date:
Hometown:

Message:

Name:
Date:
Hometown:

Message:

Name:
Date:
Hometown:

Message:

Name:
Date:
Hometown:

Message:

Name:
Date:
Hometown:

Message:

Name:
Date:
Hometown:

Message:

Name:
Date:
Hometown:

Message:

Name:
Date:
Hometown:

Message:

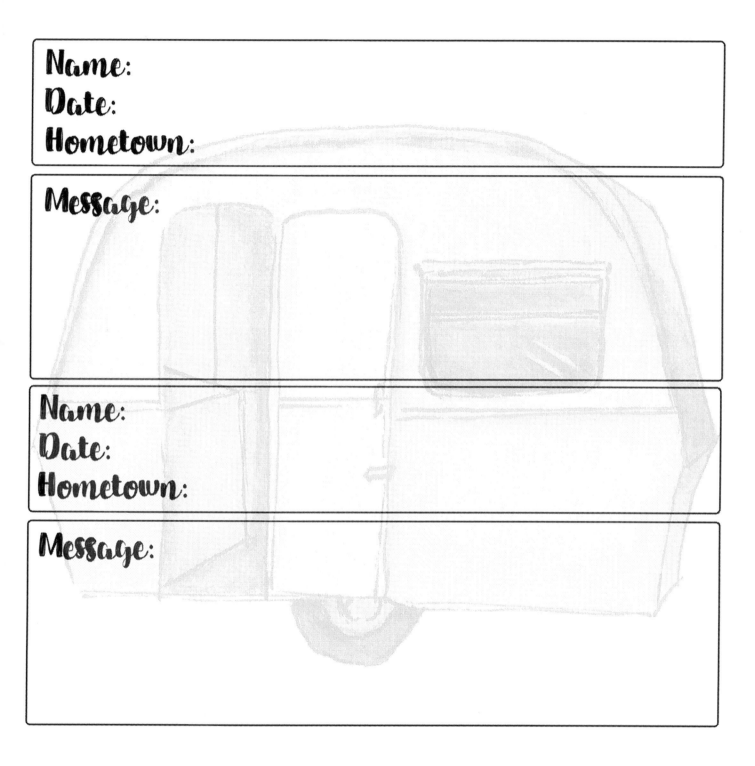

Name:
Date:
Hometown:

Message:

Name:
Date:
Hometown:

Message:

Name:
Date:
Hometown:

Message:

Name:
Date:
Hometown:

Message:

Name:
Date:
Hometown:

Message:

Name:
Date:
Hometown:

Message:

Name:
Date:
Hometown:

Message:

Name:
Date:
Hometown:

Message:

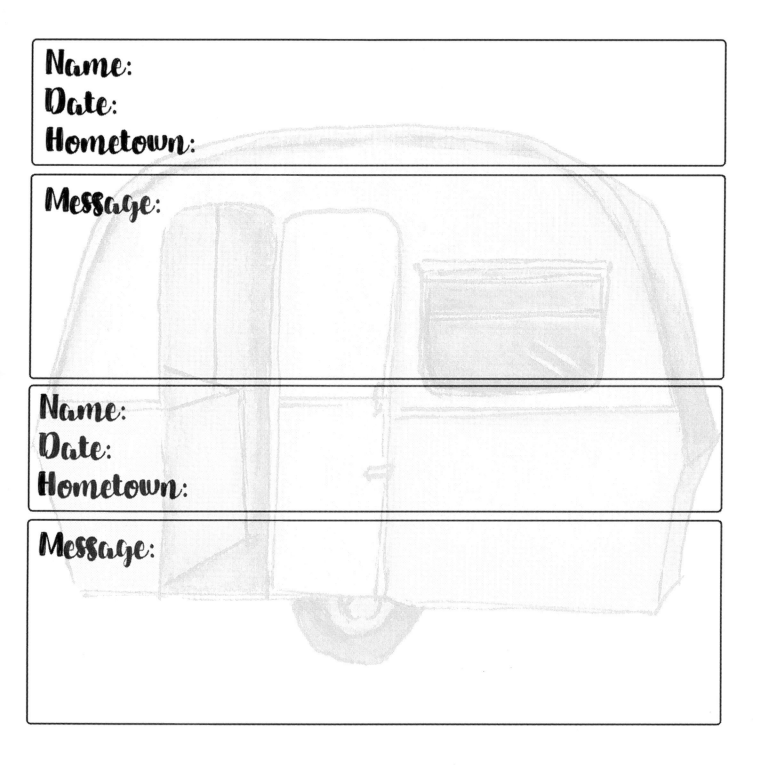

Name:
Date:
Hometown:

Message:

Name:
Date:
Hometown:

Message:

Name:
Date:
Hometown:

Message:

Name:
Date:
Hometown:

Message:

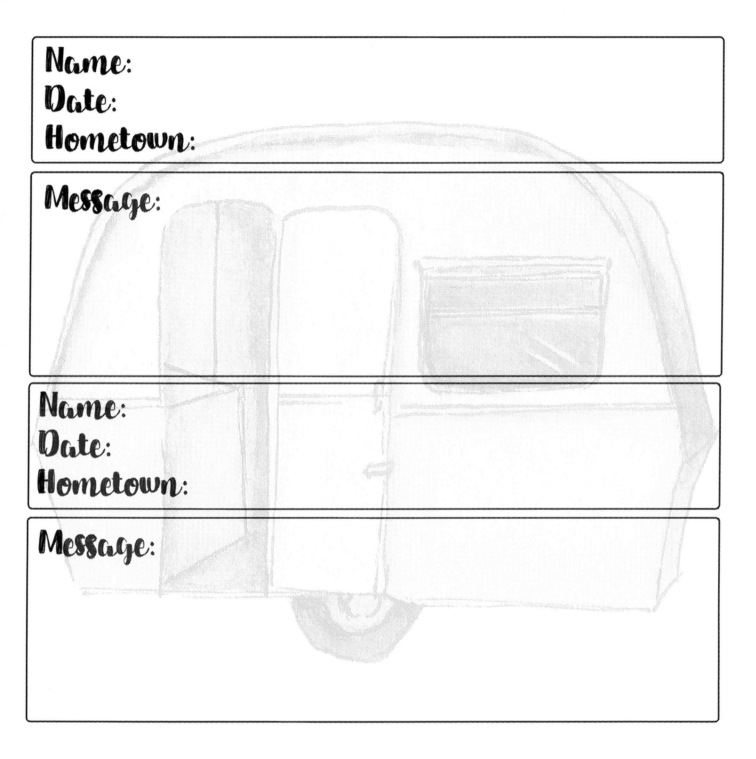

Name:
Date:
Hometown:

Message:

Name:
Date:
Hometown:

Message:

Name:
Date:
Hometown:

Message:

Name:
Date:
Hometown:

Message:

Name:
Date:
Hometown:

Message:

Name:
Date:
Hometown:

Message:

Name:
Date:
Hometown:

Message:

Name:
Date:
Hometown:

Message:

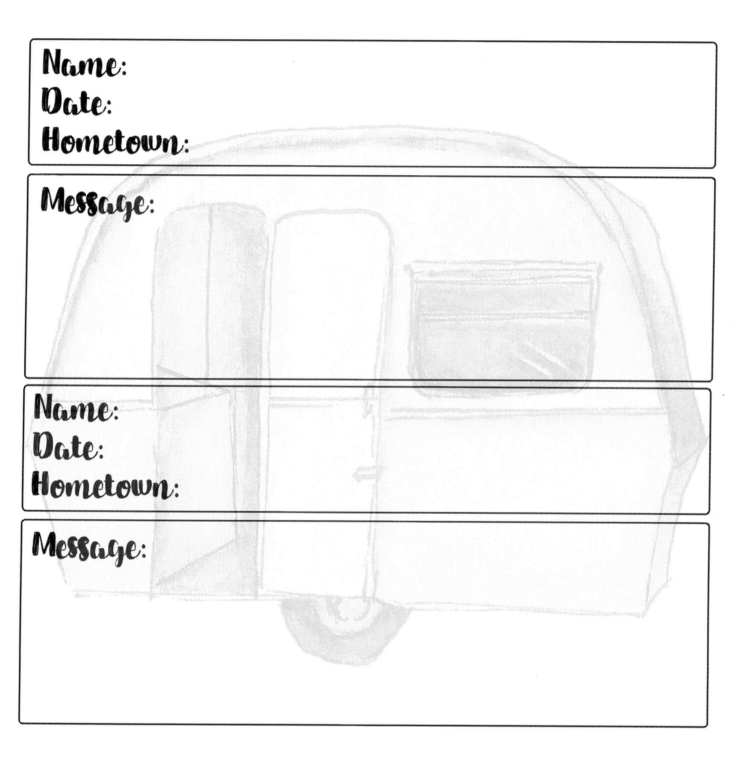

Name:
Date:
Hometown:

Message:

Name:
Date:
Hometown:

Message:

Name:
Date:
Hometown:

Message:

Name:
Date:
Hometown:

Message:

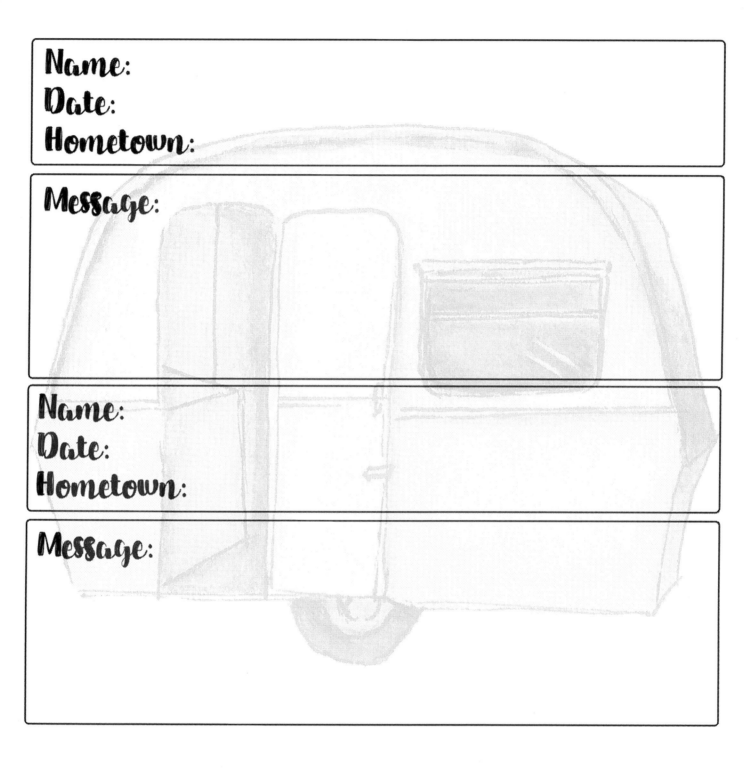

Name:
Date:
Hometown:

Message:

Name:
Date:
Hometown:

Message:

Name:
Date:
Hometown:

Message:

Name:
Date:
Hometown:

Message:

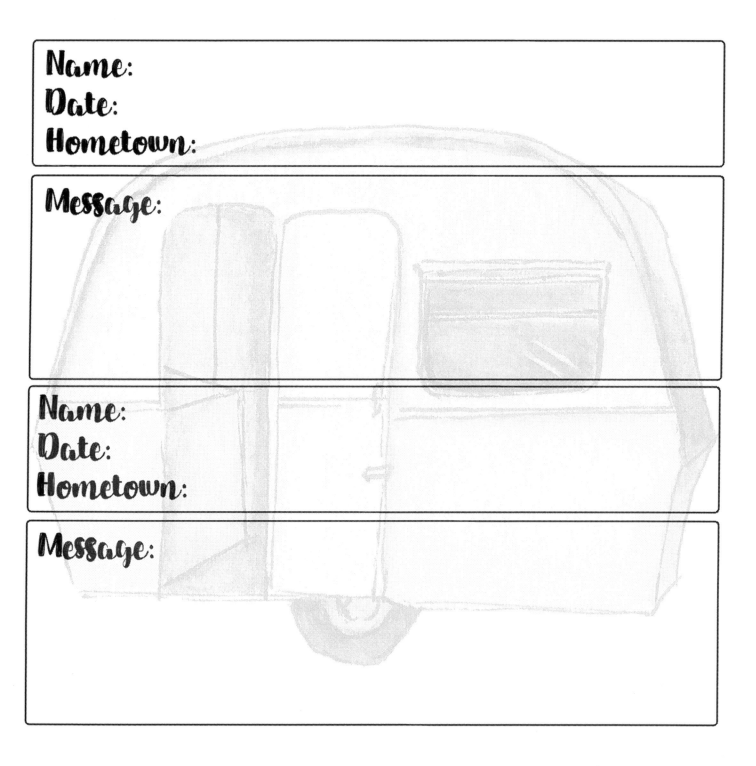

Name:
Date:
Hometown:

Message:

Name:
Date:
Hometown:

Message:

Name:
Date:
Hometown:

Message:

Name:
Date:
Hometown:

Message:

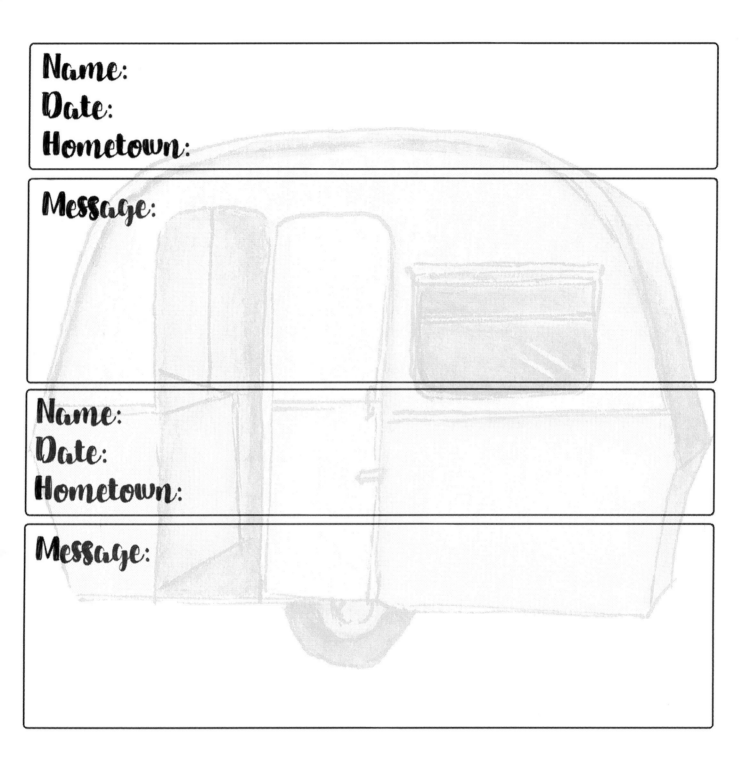

Name:
Date:
Hometown:

Message:

Name:
Date:
Hometown:

Message:

Name:
Date:
Hometown:

Message:

Name:
Date:
Hometown:

Message:

Name:
Date:
Hometown:

Message:

Name:
Date:
Hometown:

Message:

Name:
Date:
Hometown:

Message:

Name:
Date:
Hometown:

Message:

Name:
Date:
Hometown:

Message:

Name:
Date:
Hometown:

Message:

Name:
Date:
Hometown:

Message:

Name:
Date:
Hometown:

Message:

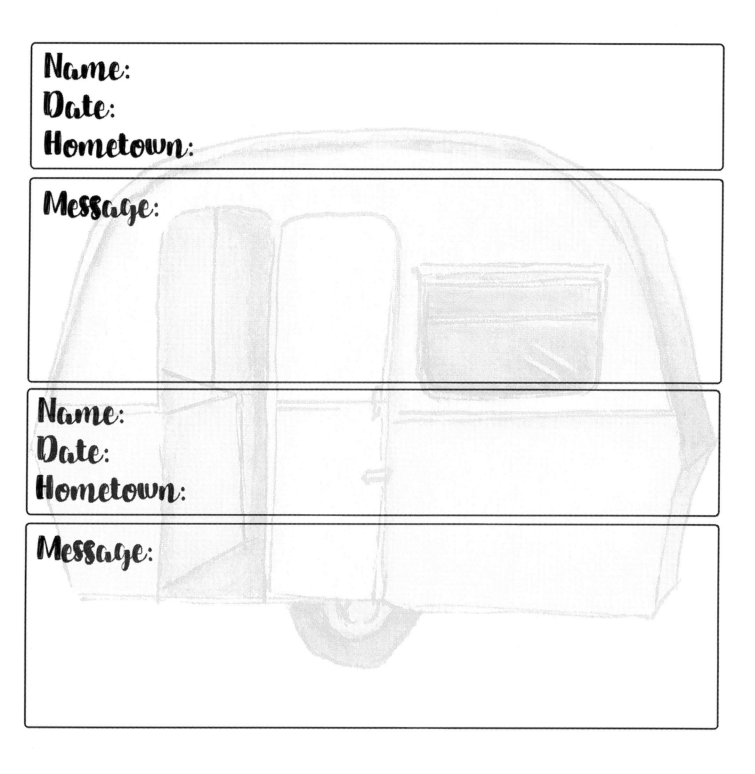

Name:
Date:
Hometown:

Message:

Name:
Date:
Hometown:

Message:

Name:
Date:
Hometown:

Message:

Name:
Date:
Hometown:

Message:

Made in the USA
Columbia, SC
05 June 2025